낭독하는 명작동화

Level 3-1

Aladdin

✦⊪ 알라딘 ⊪✦

새벽달(남수진) • 이현석 지음

롱테일
북스

Key Vocabulary

명작동화를 읽기 전에 스토리의 **핵심 단어**를
확인해 보세요. 내가 알고 있는 단어라면 체크
표시하고, 모르는 단어는 이야기를 읽은 후에 체크
표시해 보세요.

Story

Level 3의 영어 텍스트 수준은 책의 난이도를
측정하는 레벨 지수인 **AR(Accelerated
Reader) 지수 2.5~3.3 사이**로 **미국 초등
학생 2~3학년 수준**으로 맞추고, 분량을 **1100
단어 내외**로 구성했습니다.

쉬운 단어와 간결한 문장으로 구성된 스토리를
그림과 함께 읽어 보세요. 페이지마다 내용 이해를
돕는 그림이 있어 상상력을 풍부하게 해 주며,
이야기를 더욱 재미있게 읽을 수 있습니다.

Reading Training

이현석 선생님의 **강세와 청킹 가이드**에 맞춰
명작동화를 낭독해 보세요.

한국어 번역으로 내용을 확인하고 **우리말 낭독**을
하는 것도 좋습니다.

This Book

Storytelling

명작동화의 내용을 떠올릴 수 있는 **8개의 그림**이 준비되어 있습니다. 각 그림당 제시된 **3개의 단어**를 활용하여 이야기를 만들고 말해 보세요. 상상력과 창의력을 기르는 데 큰 도움이 될 것입니다.

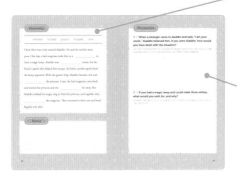

Summary

명작동화의 **줄거리 요약문**이 제시되어 있습니다. 빈칸에 들어갈 단어를 채워 보며 이야기의 내용을 다시 정리해 보세요.

Discussion

명작동화의 내용을 실생활에 응용하거나 비판적으로 생각해 볼 수 있는 **토론 질문**으로 구성했습니다. 영어 또는 우리말로 토론하며 책의 내용을 재구성해 보세요.

픽처 텔링 카드

특별부록으로 **16장의 이야기 그림 카드**가 맨 뒷장에 있어 한 장씩 뜯어서 활용이 가능합니다. 순서에 맞게 그림을 배열하고 이야기 말하기를 해 보세요.

QR코드 영상을 통해 새벽달님과 이현석 선생님이 이 책을 활용하는 가장 좋은 방법을 직접 설명해 드립니다!

Contents

Level 3-1

Aladdin

✦⊪• 알라딘 •⊪✦

Key Vocabulary

☐	**greedy**	욕심 많은
☐	**cave**	동굴
☐	**magician**	마법사
☐	**trap**	가두다
☐	**genie**	정령, 요정
☐	**wish**	소원
☐	**dusty**	먼지가 많은
☐	**rub**	문지르다
☐	**feast**	맛있는 음식, 진수성찬
☐	**pound**	(심장이) 마구 뛰다
☐	**palace**	궁전
☐	**tray**	쟁반
☐	**kindhearted**	친절한, 마음씨 고운
☐	**merchant**	상인
☐	**gulp**	벌컥벌컥 마시다
☐	**toss**	던지다

Once there was a boy named Aladdin.
He lived with his mother in a small house.
They did not have much money.

One day, a man came to Aladdin's house.

He looked rich and greedy.

"I am your uncle. I have a special adventure for us!

If you come with me, you can be rich," said the man.

"Sure, I will go," said Aladdin.

The man and Aladdin went far away from the town.

They walked for many days.

And they came to a place with a lot of rocks.

The man stopped in front of a cave.

"Here we are," he said to Aladdin.

"This is a magical cave. There is a lot of gold in there.

Go inside the cave and find a lamp for me."

Aladdin thought about his mother.
'We need the gold,' he thought.
But he was a little scared.
The man saw Aladdin's worried face.
"I will give you a ring. This will help you," said the man.

The man moved a big rock and found the secret door.
He opened it, and Aladdin went inside.

Inside the cave, there was a garden with gold and jewels.

They were beautiful.

Aladdin felt like he was in a dream.

He picked up the jewels in the cave.

Then, he found the lamp.

Aladdin shouted, "Uncle, I found the lamp! Open the door!"

"Give me the lamp!" the man shouted.

"Open the door first," said Aladdin.

"No!" the man said angrily.

The man was actually not Aladdin's uncle.

He was a bad magician.

Aladdin was trapped in the cave.

There was no light in the cave, so Aladdin was scared.
Then he remembered the ring.
He touched it, and a genie came out!

"Hello, Aladdin," said the genie.
"Who are you?" Aladdin asked.
"I am a genie, and I can help you. What is your wish?"
"Can I wish for anything? Please, take me home," said Aladdin.

Suddenly, Aladdin was home.

He brought the lamp and the jewels with him.

His mother was happy to see him.

"Where have you been, Aladdin?" she asked.

Aladdin told her about the cave, the lamp, and the genie.

He also showed her the jewels.

Aladdin's mother saw the lamp.

'I should sell the lamp tomorrow,' she thought.

But the lamp looked old and dusty.

So Aladdin's mother rubbed the lamp to clean it.

Boom! Another genie came out.

This genie was very big.

"I am the genie of this lamp," he said. "What is your wish?"

"What should I ask for?"

Aladdin's mother asked her son.

Aladdin thought for a long time.

"My mother and I are hungry," he said.

"Give us delicious food."

The genie made a feast.

Aladdin and his mother ate until night.

The next day, Aladdin was at the market.

He saw a girl.

She was beautiful and kind.

Aladdin's heart pounded because he fell in love with her.

But she was a royal princess.

And Aladdin was not a prince.

Still, Aladdin thought about her every day.

"Mother, I want to marry the princess," said Aladdin.

His mother laughed and said,

"You cannot marry her because we are not rich."

"Then take the jewels to the king," said Aladdin.

Aladdin's mother took the jewels to the king.

She had to wait for many hours.

Finally, the king met her.

'Who is this woman? Her clothes look dirty,' the king thought.

"My son would like to marry your daughter,"

said Aladdin's mother.

Then, she showed the jewels to the king.

The king was surprised, but he liked the jewels.

'How can this woman have these jewels?' he thought.

"I will think about it.

Come back after three months," said the king.

After three months, Aladdin's mother went back to the palace.

The king said, "Give me forty trays of jewels."

Aladdin's mother's heart was heavy.

So she slowly walked back home.

"The king wants forty trays of jewels," she told Aladdin.

Aladdin rubbed the lamp and called the genie.

"Genie, please give me forty trays of jewels," said Aladdin.
The genie nodded and gave Aladdin the jewels.

Aladdin's mother took the jewels to the king.
The king was surprised, but he said,
"Now, my daughter needs a palace.
It must be bigger than my palace."

Aladdin's mother told Aladdin about the palace.
Aladdin rubbed the lamp and said,
"Genie, I need a big palace. Build it near the king's palace."

At once, a grand palace was built.
The king was amazed.
So he called his daughter.

Aladdin and the princess spent time together.
The princess liked Aladdin.
He was kind and funny.

Aladdin and the princess fell in love, and they got married.
They were kindhearted, so they helped the people in the town.

Then one day, the bad magician heard about Aladdin.
He was angry, and he wanted to steal the lamp.
The magician knew of the genie's power, so he wanted it.
Soon, he came to Aladdin's city.

The magician dressed as a rich merchant.
And he went to the market.
He shouted, "Bring your old lamps!
Then I will give you new lamps!"
People brought their old lamps.
And the magician gave them new ones.

Meanwhile, Aladdin was traveling.

The princess was at her palace.

She was looking out the window.

She saw the magician and remembered Aladdin's lamp.

'Aladdin has an old lamp,' she thought.

She did not know it was a magic lamp.

She brought it to the magician.

'Finally, the lamp is mine!' the magician thought.

The magician rubbed the lamp, and the genie came out.

"I am your master now," said the magician.

"Send the princess and the palace far away.

And bring me to that palace. I want to live with the princess."

Poof! The magician's wish came true.

After a few days, Aladdin came back.

The princess and the palace were gone!

"I must find her," said Aladdin.

He rubbed his magic ring, and the genie came out.

The genie asked, "How can I help?"

Aladdin said, "Bring me to the princess."

The genie nodded, and he brought Aladdin to the princess.

Aladdin saw the princess in the palace.
He secretly went to her and said,
"Give this drink to the magician. And let's get the lamp back."

The princess gave the drink to the magician.
"Drink this. It will be good for you," she said.
The magician gulped the drink
and fell into a deep sleep.

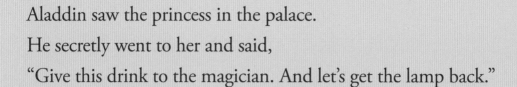

The princess quickly grabbed the lamp.
She tossed it to Aladdin, and he caught it.
Aladdin rubbed the lamp and said,
"Send us and the palace back to our city!"

The genie sent Aladdin and the princess back to their city.
Aladdin and the princess never saw the bad magician again.
And they lived happily ever after.

◆ Aladdin

Once **/** there was a **boy** named **A**laddin.

He **li**ved with his **mo**ther **/** in a **small hou**se.

They did **not** have **/** much **mo**ney.

One day, **/** a **man** **/** came to Aladdin's **hou**se.

He **look**ed **rich** **/** and **greed**y.

"I am your **un**cle. **/** I have a **spe**cial ad**ven**ture **/** for us!

If you **co**me with me, **/** you can be **rich**," **/** said the man.

"**Su**re, I will **go**," **/** said **A**laddin.

The **man** and **A**laddin **/** went **far** a**way** from the **town**.

They **walk**ed **/** for **man**y **days**.

And they **ca**me to a **place** **/** with a **lot** of **rocks**.

The **man stop**ped **/** in **front** of a **ca**ve.

"**He**re we **are**," **/** he said to **A**laddin.

"**This** is a **ma**gical **ca**ve. **/** There is a **lot** of **gold** **/** in there.

Go in**si**de the **ca**ve **/** and **find** a **lamp** for me."

◆ 알라딘

옛날에 알라딘이라는 이름의 소년이 있었습니다.
그는 자신의 어머니와 함께 작은 집에 살았어요.
그들에게는 돈이 많지 않았습니다.

어느 날, 한 남자가 알라딘의 집에 찾아왔습니다.
그는 부유하고 욕심이 많아 보였어요.
"나는 네 삼촌이야. 우리를 위한 특별한 모험이 준비되어 있단다!
네가 나를 따라온다면, 너는 부자가 될 수 있어." 남자가 말했습니다.
"좋아요, 같이 갈게요." 알라딘이 말했어요.

남자와 알라딘은 마을에서 멀리 떠났습니다.
그들은 많은 날을 걸었어요.
그리고 그들은 바위가 많이 있는 곳에 도착했습니다.

남자는 동굴 앞에서 걸음을 멈췄습니다.
"자, 여기다." 남자가 알라딘에게 말했어요.
"이것은 마법의 동굴이야. 이 안에는 많은 금이 있지.
동굴 안으로 들어가서 나에게 램프를 찾아다 줘."

Aladdin **/ thought** about his **mo**ther.

'We **need** the **gold**,' **/** he thought.

But he was a **lit**tle **sca**red.

The **man / saw** Aladdin's **wor**ried **fa**ce.

"I will **gi**ve you a **ring**. **/ This** will **help** you," **/** said the man.

The **man / mo**ved a **big rock /** and **found** the **se**cret **door**.

He **o**pened it, **/** and Aladdin **went** in**si**de.

In**si**de the **ca**ve, **/** there was a **gar**den **/** with **gold** and **je**wels.

They were **beau**tiful.

Aladdin **felt** like **/** he was in a **dream**.

He picked **up** the **je**wels **/** in the **ca**ve.

Then, **/** he **found** the **lamp**.

Aladdin **shout**ed, **/** "**Un**cle, **/** I **found** the **lamp**! **/ O**pen the **door**!"

"**Gi**ve me the **lamp**!" **/** the man **shout**ed.

"**O**pen the **door first**," **/** said A**la**ddin.

"**No**!" **/** the **man** said **an**grily.

The **man /** was **ac**tually **not** Al**a**ddin's **un**cle.

He was a **bad** ma**gi**cian.

Al**a**ddin **/** was **trap**ped in the **ca**ve.

28

알라딘은 자신의 어머니를 떠올렸습니다.
'우리는 금이 필요해.' 알라딘이 생각했어요.
하지만 그는 조금 무섭기도 했습니다.
남자는 알라딘의 걱정스러운 얼굴을 보았어요.
"내가 너에게 반지를 하나 줄게. 이 반지가 너를 도와줄 거야." 남자가 말했습니다.

남자가 커다란 바위를 치우자 비밀의 문이 나타났어요.
남자는 문을 열었고, 알라딘이 안으로 들어갔어요.

동굴 안에는, 금과 보석이 가득한 정원이 있었어요.
보물들은 아름다웠어요.
알라딘은 꿈을 꾸는 것만 같았습니다.
그는 동굴 안에 있는 보석들을 주웠습니다.
그때, 알라딘은 램프를 발견했어요.

알라딘이 소리쳤습니다. "삼촌, 제가 램프를 찾았어요! 문을 열어 주세요!"
"나에게 램프를 줘!" 남자가 외쳤어요.
"먼저 문을 열어 주세요." 알라딘이 말했습니다.
"안 돼!" 남자가 화를 내며 말했습니다.
알고 보니 남자는 알라딘의 삼촌이 아니었어요.
그는 나쁜 마법사였습니다.
알라딘은 동굴 안에 갇혔어요.

There was **no light** / in the **ca**ve, / so Aladdin was **sca**red.
Then / he re**mem**bered the **ring**.
He **touch**ed it, / and a **ge**nie came **out**!

"Hel**lo**, A**la**ddin," / said the **ge**nie.
"Who **are** you?" / A**la**ddin asked.
"I am a **ge**nie, / and I can **help** you. / **What** is your **wish**?"
"Can I **wish** for **any**thing? / **Please**, **ta**ke me **ho**me," / said A**la**ddin.

Suddenly, / A**la**ddin was **ho**me.
He **brought** / the **lamp** and the **je**wels / with him.
His **mo**ther was **hap**py / to **see** him.
"**Where** have you **been**, A**la**ddin?" / she asked.
A**la**ddin **told** her about the **ca**ve, / the **lamp**, / and the **ge**nie.
He **al**so **show**ed her / the **je**wels.

A**la**ddin's **mo**ther / **saw** the **lamp**.
'I should **sell** the **lamp** to**mor**row,' / she thought.
But the **lamp** / looked **old** and **dus**ty.
So A**la**ddin's **mo**ther / **rub**bed the **lamp** to clean it.

동굴 안에는 빛이 없어서, 알라딘은 무서웠습니다.
바로 그때 그는 반지 생각이 났어요.
알라딘은 반지를 만져 보았고, 지니가 나왔어요!

"안녕하세요, 알라딘." 지니가 말했습니다.
"너는 누구지?" 알라딘이 물었어요.
"저는 지니이고, 제가 당신을 도울 수 있어요. 당신의 소원이 뭔가요?"
"정말 아무 소원이나 말해도 돼? 부디, 나를 집으로 데려가 줘." 알라딘이 말했어요.

갑자기, 알라딘은 집에 와 있었습니다.
그는 램프와 보석들도 챙겨 왔습니다.
알라딘의 어머니는 그가 돌아와 매우 기뻤어요.
"그동안 대체 어디 있었던 거니, 알라딘?" 그녀가 물었습니다.
알라딘은 어머니에게 동굴, 램프, 그리고 지니에 대해 이야기했어요.
그는 또한 어머니에게 보석들을 보여 주었습니다.

알라딘의 어머니는 램프를 보았습니다.
'이 램프를 내일 팔아야겠다.' 그녀가 생각했어요.
하지만 램프는 낡고 먼지가 많아 보였습니다.
그래서 알라딘의 어머니는 램프를 문질러 닦았어요.

Boom! **/** An**o**ther **ge**nie **/** came **out**.

This genie **/** was **ve**ry **big**.

"I am the **ge**nie **/** of this **lamp**," **/** he said. **/** "**What** is your **wish**?"

"**What** should I **ask** for?" **/** Aladdin's **mo**ther **/ ask**ed her **son**.

Al**a**ddin **/ thought** for a **long** time.

"My **mo**ther and I are **hun**gry," **/** he said.

"**Gi**ve us de**li**cious **food**."

The **ge**nie **/ ma**de a **feast**.

Al**a**ddin and his **mo**ther **/** ate until **night**.

The **next** day, **/** Al**a**ddin was at the **mar**ket.

He **saw** a **girl**.

She was **beau**tiful **/** and **kind**.

Aladdin's **heart pound**ed **/** because he **fell** in **lo**ve with h**e**r.

But she was a **ro**yal **prin**cess.

And Al**a**ddin **/** was **not** a **prin**ce.

Still, **/** Al**a**ddin **thought** about her **/** every **day**.

짜잔! 또 다른 지니가 나왔습니다.

이 지니는 아주 컸어요.

"저는 램프의 지니랍니다." 지니가 말했습니다. "당신의 소원이 뭔가요?"

"지니에게 어떤 소원을 빌지?" 알라딘의 어머니는 아들에게 물었어요.

알라딘은 오랫동안 생각했습니다.

"엄마와 나는 배가 고파." 알라딘이 말했어요.

"우리에게 맛있는 음식을 줘."

지니는 진수성찬을 차렸어요.

알라딘과 그의 어머니는 밤늦도록 먹었습니다.

다음 날, 알라딘은 시장에 있었습니다.

그는 한 여자를 보았어요.

그녀는 아름답고 친절했습니다.

알라딘은 그녀에게 반해서 심장이 쿵쾅거렸어요.

하지만 그녀는 왕실의 공주였습니다.

그리고 알라딘은 왕자가 아니었어요.

그렇지만, 알라딘은 매일 공주를 생각했습니다.

"**Mo**ther, **/** I **want** to **mar**ry the **prin**cess," **/** said A**la**ddin.

His **mo**ther **laugh**ed and said, **/**

"You can**not mar**ry her **/** because we are **not rich**."

"**Then ta**ke the **je**wels **/** to the **king**," **/** said A**la**ddin.

A**la**ddin's **mo**ther **/ took** the **je**wels **/** to the **king**.

She **had** to **wait /** for **ma**ny **hours**.

Finally, **/** the **king met** her.

'**Who** is this **wo**man? **/** Her **clo**thes look **dir**ty,' **/** the **king** thought.

"My **son /** would like to **mar**ry your **daugh**ter," **/** said A**la**ddin's **mo**ther.

Then, **/** she **show**ed the **je**wels **/** to the **king**.

The **king** was sur**pri**sed, **/** but he **li**ked the **je**wels.

'**How** can this **wo**man **/ ha**ve these **je**wels?' **/** he thought.

"I will **think** about it.

Come **back /** after **three mon**ths," **/** said the **king**.

"어머니, 저는 공주님과 결혼하고 싶어요." 알라딘이 말했어요.
알라딘의 어머니는 웃음을 터뜨리더니 말했습니다.
"너는 공주님과 결혼할 수 없어, 우리는 부자가 아니기 때문이야."
"그럼 보석들을 국왕께 가져다드려요." 알라딘이 말했습니다.

알라딘의 어머니는 보석들을 왕에게 가져갔습니다.
그녀는 몇 시간을 기다려야 했어요.
마침내, 왕이 그녀를 만나 주었습니다.
'이 여자는 누구지? 옷이 더러워 보이는군.' 왕은 생각했습니다.

"제 아들이 폐하의 따님과 결혼하고 싶어 합니다." 알라딘의 어머니가 말했어요.
이어서, 그녀는 왕에게 보석들을 보여 주었어요.
왕은 깜짝 놀랐지만, 보석들이 마음에 들었습니다.
'어떻게 이 여자가 이 보석들을 가지고 있을 수 있지?' 왕이 생각했어요.
"내가 생각해 보겠네.
석 달 후에 돌아오게." 왕이 말했습니다.

After **three** months, **/** Aladdin's mother **/** went **back** to the **pa**lace.

The **king** said, **/** "Give me **for**ty **trays /** of **je**wels."

Al**a**ddin's **mo**ther's **heart** was **hea**vy.

So she **slow**ly **/ walk**ed back **ho**me.

"The **king** wants **/ for**ty trays of **je**wels," **/** she told Al**a**ddin.

Al**a**ddin **rub**bed the **lamp /** and **call**ed the **ge**nie.

"**Ge**nie, **/ plea**se **gi**ve me **/ for**ty trays of **je**wels," **/** said Al**a**ddin.

The **ge**nie **nod**ded **/** and **ga**ve Al**a**ddin the **je**wels.

Al**a**ddin's **mo**ther **/ took** the **je**wels **/** to the **king**.

The **king** was sur**pri**sed, **/** but he said, **/**

"**Now**, **/** my **daugh**ter **/ needs** a **pa**lace.

It **must** be **big**ger **/** than **my pa**lace."

Al**a**ddin's **mo**ther told Al**a**ddin **/** about the **pa**lace.

Al**a**ddin **/ rub**bed the **lamp** and said, **/** "**Ge**nie, **/** I **need** a **big pa**lace.

Build it **/** near the **king**'s **pa**lace."

석 달 후, 알라딘의 어머니는 다시 궁전으로 갔습니다.
왕이 말했어요. "나에게 보석 마흔 접시를 바치게."
알라딘의 어머니는 마음이 무거웠습니다.
그래서 천천히 걸어서 집으로 돌아갔어요.
"폐하께서 보석 마흔 접시를 원하셔." 그녀가 알라딘에게 말했습니다.
알라딘은 램프를 문질러서 지니를 불렀어요.

"지니, 부디 나에게 보석 마흔 접시를 줘." 알라딘이 말했습니다.
지니는 고개를 끄덕이고서는 알라딘에게 보석들을 주었어요.

알라딘의 어머니는 보석들을 왕에게 가져갔습니다.
왕은 놀랐지만, 이렇게 말했어요.
"이제, 내 딸에게는 궁전이 필요하네.
그 궁전은 내 궁전보다 커야 하네."

알라딘의 어머니는 알라딘에게 궁전에 대해 말했습니다.
알라딘은 램프를 문지르며 말했어요. "지니, 나는 커다란 궁전이 필요해.
그 궁전을 국왕의 궁전 근처에 지어 줘."

At **on**ce, **/** a **grand pa**lace was **built**.
The **king /** was a**ma**zed.
So he **call**ed his **daugh**ter.

A**la**ddin and the **prin**cess **/ spent ti**me to**ge**ther.
The **prin**cess **li**ked A**la**ddin.
He was **kind /** and **fun**ny.

A**la**ddin and the **prin**cess **fell** in **lo**ve, **/** and they got **mar**ried.
They were kind**heart**ed, **/** so they **help**ed the **peo**ple **/** in the **town**.

Then **one** day, **/** the **bad** ma**gi**cian **/ heard** about A**la**ddin.
He was **an**gry, **/** and he **want**ed to **steal /** the **lamp**.
The ma**gi**cian **/ knew** of the **ge**nie's **po**wer, **/** so he **want**ed it.
Soon, **/** he **ca**me to A**la**ddin's **ci**ty.

The ma**gi**cian **/ dress**ed as a **rich mer**chant.
And he **went** to the **mar**ket.
He **shout**ed, **/** "**Bring** your **old lamps**!
Then / I will **gi**ve you **new lamps**!"
People **brought /** their **old lamps**.
And the ma**gi**cian **/ ga**ve them **new** ones.

곧바로, 거대한 궁전이 지어졌습니다.
왕은 감탄했어요.
그래서 그는 자신의 딸을 불렀습니다.

알라딘과 공주는 함께 시간을 보냈습니다.
공주는 알라딘이 마음에 들었어요.
그는 친절하고 재미있는 사람이었거든요.

알라딘과 공주는 사랑에 빠졌고, 이내 결혼을 했습니다.
그들은 마음씨가 착해서 마을 사람들을 도왔어요.

그러던 어느 날, 나쁜 마법사가 알라딘의 소식을 들었습니다.
그는 화가 났고, 램프를 훔치고 싶었어요.
그는 지니의 능력에 대해 알고 있었고, 그 능력을 원했거든요.
곧, 마법사는 알라딘의 도시로 찾아왔습니다.

마법사는 부유한 상인처럼 차려입었습니다.
그리고 그는 시장으로 갔어요.
마법사가 외쳤습니다. "여러분의 낡은 램프를 가져오세요!
그러면 제가 여러분에게 새 램프를 드리겠습니다!"
사람들이 낡은 램프를 가져왔습니다.
그리고 마법사는 그들에게 새 램프를 주었어요.

Meanwhile, / Aladdin was traveling.

The princess / was at her palace.

She was looking out / the window.

She saw the magician / and remembered Aladdin's lamp.

'Aladdin has an old lamp,' / she thought.

She did not know / it was a magic lamp.

She brought it / to the magician.

'Finally, / the lamp is mine!' / the magician thought.

The magician rubbed the lamp, / and the genie came out.

"I am your master now," / said the magician.

"Send the princess / and the palace / far away.

And bring me / to that palace. / I want to live / with the princess."

Poof! / The magician's wish / came true.

After a few days, / Aladdin came back.

The princess and the palace / were gone!

"I must find her," / said Aladdin.

He rubbed his magic ring, / and the genie came out.

한편, 알라딘은 여행을 하고 있었습니다.
공주는 자신의 궁전에 있었어요.
공주는 창밖을 내다보고 있었습니다.
그녀는 마법사를 보고 알라딘의 램프를 떠올렸습니다.
'알라딘이 낡은 램프를 가지고 있지.' 공주가 생각했어요.
그녀는 그것이 마법의 램프인 줄 몰랐습니다.
공주는 램프를 마법사에게 가져갔어요.
'마침내, 램프가 내 것이 되겠군!' 마법사가 생각했어요.

마법사는 램프를 문질렀고, 지니가 나왔습니다.
"내가 이제 너의 주인이다." 마법사가 말했어요.
"공주와 궁전을 멀리 보내 버려.
그리고 나도 그 궁전으로 옮겨 줘. 공주와 함께 살고 싶으니까."
휙! 마법사의 소원이 이루어졌어요.

며칠 후에, 알라딘이 돌아왔습니다.
공주와 궁전은 사라지고 없었어요!
"나는 그녀를 찾아야만 해." 알라딘이 말했습니다.
그는 마법의 반지를 문질렀고, 지니가 나왔어요.

The **ge**nie **ask**ed, **/** "**How** can I **help**?
A**la**ddin said, **/** "**Bring** me **/** to the **prin**cess."
The **ge**nie **nod**ded, **/** and he **brought** Aladdin **/** to the **prin**cess.

A**la**ddin **saw** the **prin**cess **/** in the **pa**lace.
He **se**cretly **went** to her **/** and said, **/** "**Gi**ve this **drink** **/** to the ma**gi**cian.
And **let's** get the **lamp back**."

The **prin**cess **/** **ga**ve the **drink** **/** to the ma**gi**cian.
"**Drink** this. **/** It will be **good** for you," **/** she said.
The ma**gi**cian **/** **gulp**ed the **drink** **/** and **fell** into a **deep sleep**.

The **prin**cess **/** **quick**ly **grab**bed the **lamp**.
She **toss**ed it to A**la**ddin, **/** and he **caught** it.
A**la**ddin **rub**bed the **lamp** **/** and said, **/**
"**Send** us and the **pa**lace **/** **back** to our **ci**ty!"

The **ge**nie **/** **sent** Aladdin and the **prin**cess **/** **back** to their **ci**ty.
Aladdin and the **prin**cess **/** **ne**ver **saw** the **bad** ma**gi**cian a**gain**.
And they **li**ved **hap**pily ever **af**ter.

지니가 물었습니다. "제가 어떻게 도와드릴까요?"
알라딘이 말했어요. "나를 공주님께 데려가 줘."
지니는 고개를 끄덕였고, 알라딘을 공주에게 데려다주었어요.

알라딘은 성 안에 있는 공주를 보았습니다.
그는 몰래 공주에게 가서 말했습니다. "이 음료를 마법사에게 줘요.
그리고 램프를 되찾아 옵시다."

공주는 음료를 마법사에게 건네주었습니다.
"이걸 마셔 봐요. 몸에 좋을 거예요." 공주가 말했습니다.
마법사는 음료를 벌컥벌컥 마시고는 깊은 잠에 빠졌습니다.

공주는 재빨리 램프를 낚아챘어요.
공주는 램프를 알라딘에게 던졌고, 그가 받았습니다.
알라딘은 램프를 문지르며 말했습니다.
"우리와 궁전을 원래 도시로 옮겨 줘!"

지니는 알라딘과 공주를 그들의 원래 도시로 옮겨 놓았습니다.
알라딘과 공주는 다시는 나쁜 마법사와 마주치지 않았어요.
그리고 그들은 오래오래 행복하게 살았답니다.

Part 1 ◆ p.8~17

Aladdin, rich, uncle

cave, gold, lamp

ring, genie, wish

princess, jewels, king

rub, palace, marry

magician, steal, merchant

gone, find, bring

gulp, sleep, send

married   tricked   palace   trapped   cave

Once there was a boy named Aladdin. He and his mother were

poor. One day, a bad magician took him to a _____ to

find a magic lamp. Aladdin was _____ inside, but he

found a genie who helped him escape. At home, another genie from

the lamp appeared. With the genie's help, Aladdin became rich and

_____ the princess. Later, the bad magician came back

and moved the princess and the _____ far away. But

Aladdin rubbed his magic ring to find the princess, and together they

_____ the magician. They returned to their city and lived

happily ever after.

Memo

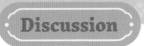

1 ◆ **When a stranger came to Aladdin and said, "I am your uncle," Aladdin believed him. If you were Aladdin, how would you have dealt with the situation?**

낯선 사람이 다가와 알라딘에게 "나는 네 삼촌이야."라고 말했을 때, 알라딘은 확인도 해 보지 않은 채 그 말을 곧이곧대로 믿었습니다. 만약 여러분이 알라딘이라면 이런 상황에서 어떻게 대처했을까요?

2 ◆ **If you had a magic lamp and could make three wishes, what would you wish for, and why?**

여러분에게 마법의 램프가 있고 세 가지 소원을 빌 수 있다면, 여러분은 어떤 소원을 빌고 싶나요? 그리고 그 이유는 무엇인가요?

낭독하는 명작동화 ⬤Level 3-1⬤
Aladdin

초판 1쇄 발행 2024년 12월 2일

지은이 새벽달(남수진) 이현석 롱테일 교육 연구소
책임편집 강지희 | **편집** 명채린 백지연 홍하늘
디자인 박새롬 | **그림** 김주연
마케팅 두잉글 사업본부

펴낸이 이수영
펴낸곳 롱테일북스
출판등록 제2015-000191호
주소 04033 서울특별시 마포구 양화로 113, 3층(서교동, 순흥빌딩)
전자메일 team@ltinc.net

이 도서는 대한민국에서 제작되었습니다.
롱테일북스는 롱테일㈜의 출판 브랜드입니다.

ISBN 979-11-93992-25-8 14740

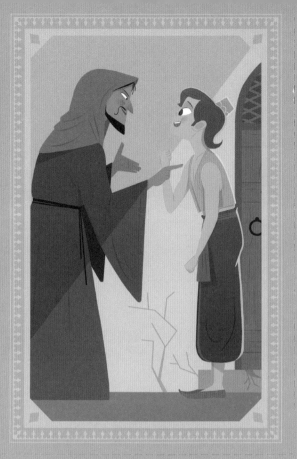

Aladdin

2

cave
gold
door

새벽달 X 이현석 낭독스쿨

Aladdin

1

rich
greedy
adventure

새벽달 X 이현석 낭독스쿨

Aladdin

4

ring
genie
wish

새벽달 X 이현석 낭독스쿨

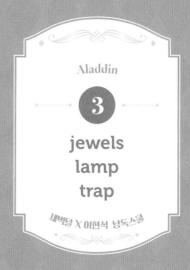

Aladdin

3

jewels
lamp
trap

새벽달 X 이현석 낭독스쿨

Aladdin

6

genie
hungry
feast

새벽달 X 이현석 낭독스쿨

Aladdin

5

mother
sell
rub

새벽달 X 이현석 낭독스쿨

Aladdin

8

jewels
king
surprised

새벽달 X 이현석 낭독스쿨

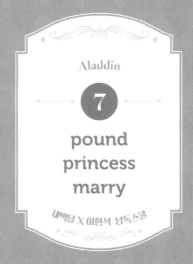

Aladdin

7

pound
princess
marry

새벽달 X 이현석 낭독스쿨

Aladdin

10

genie
jewels
palace

새벽달 X 이현석 낭독스쿨

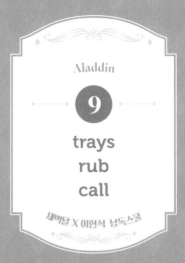

Aladdin

9

trays
rub
call

새벽달 X 이현석 낭독스쿨

Aladdin

12

steal
merchant
market

새벽달 X 이현석 낭독스쿨

Aladdin

11

build
daughter
kindhearted

새벽달 X 이현석 낭독스쿨

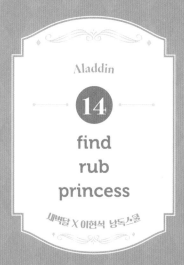

Aladdin

14

find
rub
princess

새벽달 X 이현석 낭독스쿨

Aladdin

13

magician
bring
send

새벽달 X 이현석 낭독스쿨

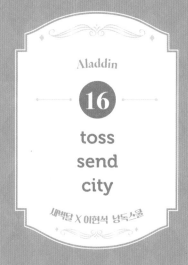

Aladdin

16

toss
send
city

새벽달 X 이현석 낭독스쿨

Aladdin

15

drink
gulp
sleep

새벽달 X 이현석 낭독스쿨